OCTOPUS
OCEAN

Geniuses of the Deep

OCTOPUS OCEAN

Geniuses of the Deep

MARK LEIREN-YOUNG

ORCA BOOK PUBLISHERS

Published in Canada and the United States in 2025 by Orca Book Publishers.
orcabook.com

Library and Archives Canada Cataloguing in Publication
Title: Octopus ocean : geniuses of the deep / Mark Leiren-Young.
Names: Leiren-Young, Mark, author.
Series: Orca wild ; 16.
Description: Series statement: Orca wild ; 16 | Includes bibliographical references and index.
Identifiers: Canadiana (print) 20240345819 | Canadiana (ebook) 20240345827 |
ISBN 9781459838956 (hardcover) | ISBN 9781459838970 (EPUB) | ISBN 9781459838963 (PDF)
Subjects: LCSH: Octopuses—Juvenile literature. | LCSH: Octopuses—Conservation—
Juvenile literature. | LCGFT: Instructional and educational works.
Classification: LCC QL430.3.O2 L45 2025 | DDC j594/.56—DC23

Library of Congress Control Number: 2024934925

Summary: Part of the nonfiction Orca Wild series for middle-grade readers and illustrated
with color photographs throughout, this book introduces kids to octopuses all over the
world. It discusses octopus habitat, biology and threats to survival, and how scientists,
conservationists and young people are working to protect octopuses everywhere.

Orca Book Publishers is committed to reducing the consumption of
nonrenewable resources in the production of our books. We make
every effort to use materials that support a sustainable future.

Orca Book Publishers gratefully acknowledges the support for its publishing
programs provided by the following agencies: the Government of Canada,
the Canada Council for the Arts and the Province of British Columbia
through the BC Arts Council and the Book Publishing Tax Credit.

Front and back cover photo by
Reynold Mainse/Design Pics/Getty Images.
Design by Troy Cunningham.
Edited by Kirstie Hudson.

Printed and bound in South Korea.

28   27   26   25   •   1   2   3   4

BUENA VISTA IMAGES/GETTY IMAGES

For Rayne Benu, who told me
I had to write about octopuses
because they're amazing. She was
right. They are. For my mom who
first introduced me to an octopus.
And for everyone interested
in the underwater world.

Contents

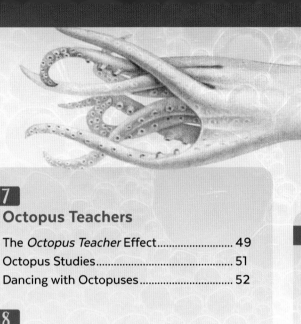

A giant Pacific octopus—the same species as Storm—checks out the view from a tank.

MARK NEWMAN/GETTY IMAGES

INTRODUCTION

OCTOPUS TEACHING

A young octopus named Storm just shook my hand, and as I write this my fingers are still tingling. While Storm's body was wrapped around the little red rock crab she'd captured for dinner, one arm tentatively reached out to consider the new human standing at the top of her tank. Me.

I was being supervised by marine biologist Kit Thornton. She's in charge of animal care at the Shaw Centre for the Salish Sea where this giant Pacific octopus has lived for just under six months. Before dipping a hand in the tank, I had to rinse off any traces of the outside world in a small trough of sea water. It was feeding time for the octopus, and she only eats every two or three days. After a meal Storm basically naps until it's time to eat again.

A stuffed toy octopus guards the door at the Salish Sea Centre.

MARK LEIREN-YOUNG

IN-FLIGHT OCTOPUS

One of the best part of writing books is getting to go behind the scenes at places like aquariums. I'd watched Storm and several other octopuses who'd lived at the Salish Sea Centre. But I'd never been in the back room and taken the hidden stairs to reach inside the tank.

In the winter of 2022, Storm was set to fly from Vancouver Island to an aquarium in Finland. A storm delayed her trip. She needed a place to wait out the weather and ended up in the nearest aquarium to her ocean home—the Salish Sea Centre in Sidney, British Columbia. Because of the delay, the aquarium team in Finland decided to find a new octopus. Since Storm was stuck in Sidney because of the wild winter weather, a name for her was obvious.

If she'd made her epic flight, Storm would have spent her entire life—possibly as long as five years—in the Finnish aquarium. The Salish Sea Centre only keeps octopuses on display for about six months before returning them to the ocean. So Kit and her colleagues don't want their octopuses to get comfortable with too many humans, which is why I'm honored to be invited to meet Storm.

BEHIND THE TANK

After undoing the four latches on the wooden lid to slide open the tank, Kit splashes the water to say hi to Storm. The octopus doesn't move. Kit has met 11 giant Pacific octopuses, four ruby octopuses and four common octopuses. They all have different personalities. As octopuses go, Storm is not a rock star. She is more likely to hide behind a rock than put on a show.

Other residents of the same 2,300-gallon (8,700-liter) tank would greet the people feeding them, maybe play with them. The previous octopus-in-residence, Sequin, would visit her keepers before being fed. Or she might swim over to see them right after catching her meal, to show off her prize. Almost every time I saw Sequin, she was doing something. Whenever I'd seen Storm—from the earliest days of her arrival—she was about as active as an anemone.

Storm does not find us interesting. Or she's not curious about Kit at the moment. Or me. She stays attached to the window of her tank, thinking her octopus thoughts. Kit drops a live crab into the water. Storm is on top of her meal in a second. Octopuses can go from zero to *Wow, did you see that?* in a flash. Some people outside her tank scream.

OCTOPUS IN ACTION

Her speed shocks me. This is my first time seeing an octopus move with intent. I'd never realized how quickly they can do whatever it is they want to do. Watching an octopus is like watching a dream. They look as if they're

Storm's suckers hold on to the glass in her tank at the Salish Sea Centre.
MARK LEIREN-YOUNG

3

Storm being a star
with a starfish at the
Salish Sea Centre.
MARK LEIREN-YOUNG

drifting like jellyfish until they want to get somewhere, and then they jet through the water.

As Storm covers the crab with her body, her arms extend. Suddenly I realize that what I thought was a small octopus is about six and a half feet (two meters) from the tip of one arm to the tip of another. Then Storm retracts her arms and returns to the side of her tank.

Kit tries to get Storm's attention again but doesn't expect a visit. She's about to surrender when one of the eight arms pulls away from the others. It drifts toward us, looking more like the leaf of a plant than the limb of an animal. A second arm stretches out. If an arm could talk, I suspect it would say, "What do you want? I'm eating."

Kit tells me I can put my hand in the water. I do, and the tip of an octopus arm unspools, reaches out and wraps around my smallest two fingers. Two small suckers—the size of cherry pits—attach to me.

Her arm is soft and silky and feels the way I imagine a jellyfish would—like it's barely there. The suction cups are tiny, cute, powerful and loaded with sensory receptors. The suckers not only hold things but taste them. Storm's deciding whether I'm friend, foe or food. She is being very gentle, and for an animal who can crush a crab's shell, gentle is a choice. After maybe a minute of checking me out, it's clear to Storm that I am not as interesting as her crab. She lets me go, and the stray arm returns to her side.

MY FIRST OCTOPUS

The first octopus I saw was at the Vancouver Aquarium when I was four or five. I was fascinated by how well it could hide. That was before I learned that octopuses are the animal kingdom's greatest escape artists, and before scientists realized how smart they are. I never imagined I'd get to meet one or share their stories.

One of the most exciting things about exploring the world of octopuses is that we are learning something new about them almost every day. This book is full of discoveries made while I was writing it. And many of these discoveries have sparked more questions than answers. I hope this book answers some of your questions about octopuses—and inspires you to ask even more.

Let's dive in…

A giant Pacific octopus keeping an eye on us.
GREG AMPTMAN/SHUTTERSTOCK.COM

A day octopus near Kona,
the Big Island, Hawaii.
STUART WESTMORLAND/GETTY IMAGES

1

EIGHT LIVES

The more I learn about octopuses, the more convinced I am that if fish had superheroes, every trout, darter and herring would want to be bitten by a radioactive octopus. An octopus has the skills to be a superhero, superspy or super-criminal. They are escape artists, masters of disguise, able to hide almost anywhere, and, most amazingly, are born brilliant. Octopuses aren't taught anything by their parents. When they hatch—and they are born in eggs—they discover the oceans on their own.

> "We know how amazingly intelligent the octopus is—and they don't even have a normal brain, more like a central nervous system."
>
> —Jane Goodall, primatologist and environmental leader

All arms on deck! A giant Pacific octopus explores a small tank.

OCTOPUSES IN AQUARIUMS

If you've seen an octopus at an aquarium, it's likely you've met a giant Pacific octopus. These are a favorite animal of exhibitors because of their impressive size and lifespan. They can survive almost five years, which is a long time for an octopus.

There are at least 300 other kinds of octopuses, and they live in every ocean. They don't live in fresh water. We don't know exactly how many species there are and likely never will. That's because oceans cover most of the planet and are still largely unexplored, and some octopuses are tinier than your eyeball. Also, if there were a world championship for hide-and-seek, the octopus would win all the gold medals and then stash them somewhere they'd never be found.

OCTOPUSES EVERYWHERE?

The day I was writing this, scientists discovered a new species of octopus in the ocean near an extinct undersea volcano off the coast of Costa Rica. This small octopus (the body is about the size of a baseball) doesn't have an official name yet.

When you take a break from reading this book, please do a search on a computer using the words *new octopus discovered*. I suspect there will be at least one story about an amazing octopus that someone learned about since I wrote these words. Maybe since you started reading them. But a species being new to scientists doesn't mean it's new to people who live near the water. A "new" octopus is certainly not new to their prey or predators.

INK SPOTS.

DISCOVERING THE DORADO

In early 2024 a group of scientists from around the world went back to visit the nurseries near Costa Rica and discovered at least four new octopus species. One is now known as the Dorado octopus, as it was first found near a rock formation called the Dorado Outcrop. We now know that the Dorado broods in the seafloor's warm waters and that octo moms live in these nurseries year-round. The ongoing discoveries at this octopus hot spot are a reminder of how little we know about life in the ocean.

INK SPOTS.

FROM POLYPOUS TO OCTOPUS

In the 16th century the word *octopus*, or "eight foot," was created—likely by Carl Linnaeus. The Swedish botanist is famous for devising names, categories and catalogs of animals that we still use today. Linnaeus preferred Latin, but *octopus* comes from two Greek words—*okto*, meaning "eight," and *pous*, meaning "foot." The term was picked up in English about 200 years after Linnaeus used it in his books.

Pl. XXIII.   T. 2. P. 113.

LE POULPE COMMUN .

Scientists didn't manage to film a live giant squid in the wild until 2006. And that's not just one of the biggest animals on the planet but also one of the biggest animals who has ever lived on the planet. But people who spend time on and near the water have told tales of these "sea monsters" for as long as we've told tales. Not only are there many species we haven't met yet, but there are far too many species that went extinct before we started looking.

MEET THE MOLLUSKS

So who are the octopuses? Octopuses, squid and their cousins the cuttlefish are soft-bodied undersea animals known as **cephalopods**. This is a Greek word meaning "head foot." Unlike most **mollusks**, cephalopods do not have protective shells. Mollusks are **invertebrates**—animals without backbones. About 600 million years ago, animals on earth divided between vertebrates (like us) and invertebrates (like mollusks). Most animals on earth—about 98 percent—are invertebrates.

Ancient ancestors of cephalopods had shells but eventually evolved out of them. They lost the protection in favor of speed, flexibility and their many magical moves. Most octopuses hang out on or near the bottom of the oceans. Some live closer to shore. A few live near the surface. Floating octopuses are **pelagic**—which means they live in the open ocean, not on the seafloor.

An octopus in the purple
glow of a neon light.
KATOOSHA/GETTY IMAGES

WHO OR WHAT IS AN OCTOPUS?

In most books about animals, an octopus like Storm would
be referred to as a what, not a who. It, not she. Historically,
anything nonhuman—whether an animal or this book—is
grammatically and philosophically considered a thing. I
refer to animals the same way I refer to humans—as who,
not what, and as he/she/they, not it. One of my heroes, the
legendary environmentalist Jane Goodall, also does this
and urges everyone to do the same.

In the case of octopuses and other invertebrates,
reminding people that they are living beings like us is especially important and, surprisingly, political. In the United
States, octopuses and other invertebrates are not currently
considered animals—they are legally things. That means
they have no rights or legal protections.

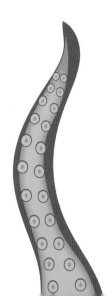

11

INK SPOTS.

THINK INK

Octopuses make chameleons look like amateurs at camouflage. Octopuses can change colors faster than any lizard, and most can shift not just the color of their skin but the texture too. Octopuses also have the ability to shoot ink from their bodies. Cephalopod ink makes these animals not only harder to see but also harder to smell. All octopuses we know of (except the dumbo and the banded string-arm) are born with ink sacs, and even a baby octopus can spray ink.

OCTOPUSES AND OCTOPI

I was taught that the plural of *octopus* is **octopi**. It's not, even though you'll still find *octopi* in dictionaries. *Octopus* is a Latin version of a Greek word. Using *i* at the end of a word is a tradition for Latin terms. For Greek words the tradition is to use an *s*. So the word scientists use for more than one octopus isn't *octopi*—though it does sound cool—but *octopuses*. A formal Greek plural would be *octopodes*—which is used by pretty much no one.

INKY TRICKS

People used to believe that octopuses sprayed ink when they were scared or startled. This idea goes back at least as far as ancient Greece. In 350 BCE

Aristotle wrote about frightened octopuses spraying ink. The more people learned about octopuses, though, the clearer it became that spurting ink isn't a reflex but a strategy.

Ancient Greeks and Romans used cephalopod ink for painting and writing. The ink is brown but can appear black in deep water or when there's a lot of it. The ink contains *melanins*—the same color-creating pigments found in human skin. While the ink can repel and hurt some undersea animals, it's not dangerous to people. Cultures around the world have used the ink to flavor food. There have even been experiments using ink as a potential medicine.

Different species have different inks. Some squid can eject ink to create a *pseudomorph*—something that looks enough like them to fool predators. Caribbean reef squid have ink that changes their flavor to make them a lot less tasty to any animal looking to eat them. And some squid can use their ink to communicate with each other.

A deadly blue-ringed
octopus near Indonesia.
MIKAELERIKSSON/GETTY IMAGES

2
THINKING LIKE AN OCTOPUS

The most fascinating thing about octopuses isn't their exotic look—or even all those arms—but their minds. Octopuses are smart, but their brains aren't like ours or any other animal we know. Their brains—the biggest of any invertebrate—are located behind their eyes and wrap around their stomachs. So they're shaped like donuts. An octopus brain stretches when it's time to eat so they can swallow their food. Every list I've found of the smartest animals on earth includes octopuses—usually along with orcas, dolphins, elephants, pigs, ravens and various apes. Other contenders are

"What do we really know about the octopus? Nothing."

—Jennifer Mather, octopus expert

parrots, pigeons, crows, goats, rats and sometimes cats and dogs. The BBC TV series *Super Smart Animals* listed the top five as octopuses, orangutans, chimps, crows and dolphins.

OCTOPUS IQ

Most of the animals we consider intelligent (like apes, elephants and orcas) are social, have powerful family connections and live a long time. Octopuses don't have teachers. They have no family bonds and, as far as we know, don't make friends with other octopuses. Even the most long-lived species only survive for about five years—an age when a young elephant, ape, orca or human is still being taught the ways of the world. Most animals have childhoods, which is when we learn about the world and, ideally, are cared for and taught by elders. Octopuses have to understand their world as soon as they hatch.

INK SPOTS

PERSONALITY TEST

Everyone who has met more than one octopus knows that each one is an individual. Canadian scientist Jennifer Mather, one of the world's foremost octopus experts, invented a test to determine how brave or shy an octopus is. When she devised the test, it was one of the first personality studies ever done on any animals other than monkeys.

She performed several different experiments, including touching them with a test-tube brush. Did they hide from the brush? Did they attack it? Did they observe it? She also put an empty pill bottle in a tank to see if the octopus avoided it, tried to open it or played with it. She studied how octopuses approached opening clams to understand their styles of problem-solving. Jennifer told me she saw "huge differences" in individuals. She said, "They have very strong personalities."

BRAIN WAVES

A common octopus has about 500 million neurons—the parts of a brain that process information. Human brains have about 86 billion. What's unique about the neurons of an octopus is that two-thirds are in their arms. Not only can each arm take in its surroundings and process information, but each sucker has the ability to do its own thing, like our fingers can. This is especially impressive when an octopus like the giant Pacific can have more than 2,000 suckers. A study in 2023 showed that octopuses have a type of brain wave that no other animal does—including humans. And nope, we don't know what it does yet. Octopuses can use tools. They can recognize individual humans. Many of the things octopuses do to catch prey and escape predators are so complicated that humans are only now realizing how intelligent these animals truly are.

A common octopus takes a very uncommon mirror test.
CAPTAINDARWIN/WIKIMEDIA COMMONS/CC BY-SA 4.0 DEED

A coconut octopus wears shells as armor.
NICK HOBGOOD/WIKIMEDIA COMMONS/ CC BY-SA 3.0 DEED

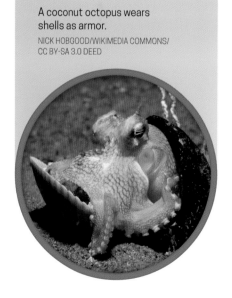

Coconut octopuses fight underwater near Bali.

A tiny octopus is squeezed inside a small rusted food can.

OCTOPUS ARMOR

Humans used to believe we were the only species smart enough to build and use tools. We now know that many animals use tools, but octopuses create tools, weapons, shelters and even armor.

Gloomy octopuses, who live near New Zealand and Australia, toss silt, shells and algae at uninvited guests approaching their homes. Some female octopuses toss objects at male octopuses when they're not interested in them as potential mates. Some male blanket octopuses and giant deep-sea octopuses use jellyfish stingers as weapons to attack and capture prey.

Several types of octopuses, including the veined or coconut octopus, use coconut shells to create undersea armor. The octopus star of the 2020 documentary *My Octopus Teacher* escapes becoming a snack for a shark by covering herself with rocks and shells. Octopuses also use our garbage—bottles, cans and other trash—as homes, hiding spots and weapons.

While octopuses don't play well with each other, some species appear to team up with other fish—like groupers—to hunt. Octopuses have also been spotted "punching" their partners or prey, or swatting at other fish, for no apparent reason.

INK SPOTS.

OCTOPUS DREAMS

Heidi, a day octopus, was asleep in a small tank in Alaska when a documentary crew saw something they couldn't explain. She began to change colors and twitch, then shot out an arm. If she were a human or a dog or one of so many other species, no one would have doubted that she was dreaming. Author and marine biologist David Scheel, who filmed the scene, believed that's what he was witnessing. Other scientists weren't sure what these movements meant. But plenty of people have seen octopuses doing what certainly looks like dreaming.

Do octopuses dream? Dreams happen when animals are in deep sleep. No one knows exactly why we sleep or why we dream. If an animal as different from us as an octopus dreams, will that tell us something new about what dreams do? Sleeping isn't safe for any animal. If we're not awake, we can't be ready for danger. But if dreams are how our brains process what we learn—which is what many scientists believe—dreaming would be as important for an octopus as it is for us, because they have to learn a lot in a very short time.

A camouflaged octopus.

3

INSIDE THE OCTOPUS

Brains everywhere. Blue blood. A beak. Three hearts. Eight arms. It's easy to understand why octopuses are the inspiration for so many aliens and monsters. They may not be from outer space, but they're less like us than almost any other animal on the planet. When I started writing about orcas—my initial dive into life in the oceans—a scientist explained that until fairly recently, most research on animals focused on how to catch them, how to eat them and what was inside them. He called this the era of slice-and-dice science. Today research focuses more

"Looking into the eyes of an octopus or squid or their frilly-skirted cousins, the cuttlefish, I get the uncanny feeling that somebody is home there, somebody who is regarding me with more than casual interest."

—Sylvia Earle, marine biologist

on animals' habits and minds, on how and why they do what they do.

BIG BRAINS AND BLUE BLOOD

A typical octopus has three hearts. Two of them move blood to the gills, and the other makes sure their blood flows through the rest of their body. Instead of red blood—like we have—octopuses are blue-blooded. This is because their blood is copper-based and our blood is mostly iron-based. Some octopus ink is poisonous and can paralyze both predators and prey. It can even kill the octopus who sprays it.

The thing that looks like an octopus head isn't a head—it's the body. Known as the *mantle*, this sack that makes up most of the octopus holds the hearts, stomach and other

A giant Pacific octopus swims in the Sea of Japan.
ANDREY NEKRASOV/ALAMY STOCK PHOTO

INK SPOTS

organs and features a pair of gill slits on either side. When an octopus wants to move quickly, they shoot water out of a tube in their body known as a *siphon*. The gills pull water in and then spray it out through the siphon.

Octopuses have eight arms, which can keep moving and feeling after being cut, bitten off or discarded to escape or distract a predator. A predator may follow an arm as it moves off on its own.

CHROMATOPHORES

Octopuses change color using **chromatophores**—small sacs of pigments in their skin that shrink or expand to shift the color being displayed based on surroundings or activity. The chromatophores contain three colors—yellow, red and brown/black—that change to create a range of colors. Changing colors isn't just about camouflage. Octopuses also change colors to communicate with potential mates and scare away other sea life.

BEAKS AND TONGUES

Octopuses and other cephalopods have beaks as birds do. Their beaks work like scissors to cut their food. They are made up of two separate pieces and can retract into their bodies like a cat's claws. Beaks are made of *chitin*—the same organic material found in the shells of bugs and crabs.

Inside an octopus beak is a rough, sharp tongue called the *radula* that is like a collection of tiny teeth. An octopus can use their radula to poke and drill holes in shells. Then there's another layer of lethal trouble for anything an octopus wants to eat. The salivary glands of an octopus have muscles around them. And toxins. Giant Pacific octopuses have two different salivary glands. One pair produces a toxin and the other produces digestive enzymes—the acid that dissolves food. The toxin can stun or kill their prey so that their food isn't fighting back when they eat it.

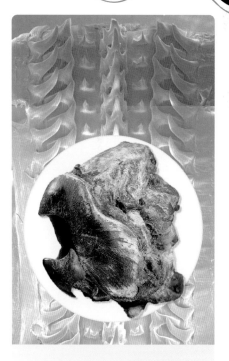

The beak of a giant Pacific octopus. The image behind is a close-up of the radula located inside the beak.
JAMES COSGROVE

INK SPOTS.

PAPILLAE

Octopuses have minuscule muscles called *papillae* that can rearrange themselves on their skin. Papillae shift to create different shapes and textures—such as bumps, spikes and ridges. This means an octopus can not only mimic the color of sand or stone or algae or coral, but also the way they look and feel. Many octopuses have horn-shaped bumps above their eyes. Canadian octopus expert James Cosgrove says he generally sees the horns when an octopus seems relaxed.

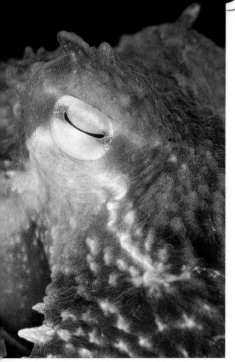

ANDREY NEKRASOV/GETTY IMAGES

Some octopuses have poison strong enough to kill humans.

The mouth that holds the beak and tongue is located under what is basically an octopus armpit—because octopuses really are that bizarre. Until recently octopuses were believed to be nocturnal hunters, but the more time humans spend with them, the less clear it is whether they stick to hunting at night.

SEEING AND HEARING

Octopuses see about as well as we do, but they don't see colors—at least, not like we do—which makes their ability to change colors even more impressive. A study in 2021 found that octopus arms can sense light even if they can't see it. It's not clear exactly how an octopus arm does this, but based on tests in which scientists cut octopuses to monitor their reactions, there seem to be sensors in the muscles.

Octopuses' pupils are shaped like rectangles. Their eyeballs don't work like ours. Most animals focus by shifting the size of the lenses in their eyes. Octopuses shift their eyeballs to focus.

Scientists used to be convinced that octopuses couldn't hear because they don't have ears or chambers like the swim bladders that fish use for registering sound. In 2009 scientists realized that octopuses and squid sense sound with organs called *statocysts*. These two small chambers, found near their brains, also help octopuses balance. They contain hairs that register vibrations, like human ears do.

Squid have a better audio sense because they have gas-filled areas in their body to amplify sound.

TASTE BY TOUCH

We taste our food with little cells on our tongues known as taste buds. Octopuses don't taste with their tongues. They use their tongues more like we use our teeth. And they use their suckers like we use our tongues. They are **chemotactic**, which means they taste food by touching it. Humans figured this out in 2023 and believe that flavor influences octopuses' approach to hunting.

Their favorite foods tend to be other animals with shells, like shrimp, crabs, clams, snails and lobsters. They also eat fish who are smaller than them, and other octopuses. They may eat every day, but some octopus species eat as infrequently as twice a week. Squid and cuttlefish have different wiring for their receptors and aren't as keen on grease. Squid pull potential food close to check it out before deciding whether to eat it.

The suckers of a giant Pacific octopus.
STUART WESTMORLAND/GETTY IMAGES

INK SPOTS.

OCTOPUS POOP

Octopus stomachs only have one tube for food to go in and out. Octopuses poop through their siphons—the same organ they use to shoot out water to propel themselves and to spray ink.

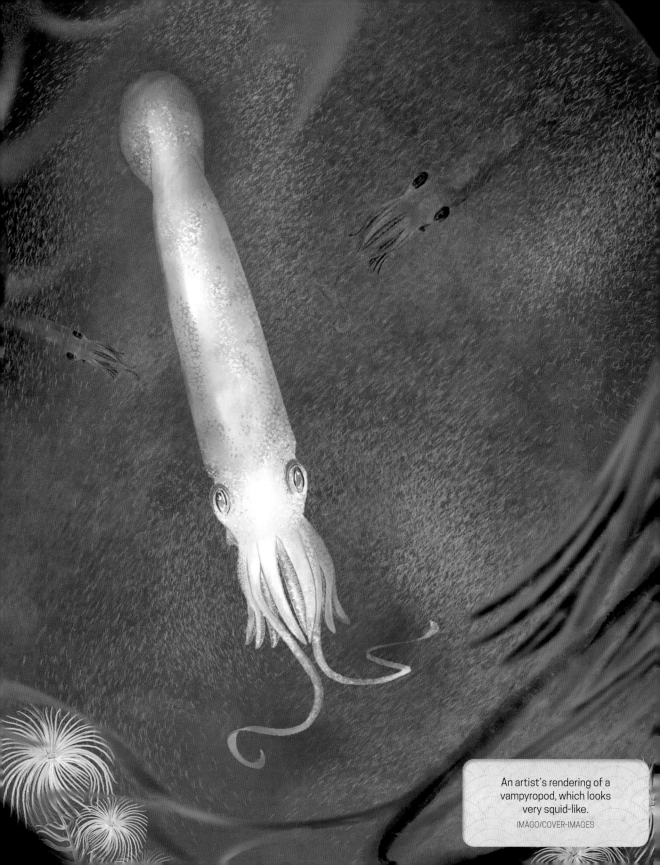

An artist's rendering of a vampyropod, which looks very squid-like.

4

THE ORIGINAL OCTOPUS

The octopus is older than almost everything else on earth. Before there were dinosaurs, before there were trees, there were ancient octopuses. *Vampyropods* were one such ancestor, though they looked more like squid than octopuses. They had 10 arms, like a squid. Two of those arms were longer than the others and were likely the primary arms.

VISITING THE VAMPYROPODS

In 2022 scientists in Canada realized how long ago vampyropods lived. Back in

> "The octopus is a stupid creature, for it will approach a man's hand if it be lowered in the water."
>
> —Aristotle, Greek philosopher

1988 the Royal Ontario Museum received a fossil specimen from Montana and put it in a drawer. More than 20 years later, a researcher took a closer look and spotted the remains of a 5-inch (12-centimeter) octopus ancestor complete with traces of what looks like an ink sac. Until they ran tests on the new discovery, the oldest known vampyropod was from a mere 240 million years ago. This one was much older—more than 330 million years old. The scientists decided to name their discovery after US president Joe Biden, supposedly not as a joke about the age of the president but as a tribute to his support for scientific research.

These octopus ancestors had shells. There are a few theories about why they lost them. One is that if they were living in deeper water, it would have been challenging to keep enough gas in the shell to remain buoyant. Shells might have slowed them down and made them easier prey for dolphins and other predators, who hunt with echolocation. Or—a current winning theory—shells weren't as useful as speed. Losing the shell meant octopuses could hunt, and hide, faster.

INK SPOTS.

SNAKESTONES

Today scientists know that one of the ancient original molluscs were what we call ammonites. Long extinct, ammonites lived in the oceans in the Jurassic era—between 240 and 66 million years ago. In medieval Europe where science and fossil identification wasn't a thing yet, ammonite fossils were dubbed snakestones because they looked like petrified snakes. These fossils were so common around Whitby in England that some people believed St. Hilda turned snakes to stone in the 7th century.

A nautilus swims in Micronesian waters.
WILDESTANIMAL/GETTY IMAGES

NAUTILUSES

Because nature and science like to keep things interesting, there's another type of cephalopod known as the *nautilus*. They've been around about 500 million years, and as I write this there are six known living species. A nautilus has a hard shell like a snail's. The shell has different compartments, and new ones are added as they grow. The animal lives in the largest one. The others hold seawater and gas that let them float and are used for movement. Nautiluses shoot water to move. They have no arms and about 90 suckerless tentacles. Scientists used to believe they were mindless, but in 2008 tests showed that a nautilus can learn to associate a blue light with food and remember this for about a day.

An empty nautilus shell.
JAMES COSGROVE

29

A belemnite fossil in a chalk stone.
ICRMS/SHUTTERSTOCK.COM

BELEMNITES

If there were an undersea version of *Jurassic Park*, belemnites were the octopus ancestors swimming during the Jurassic and Cretaceous periods—roughly 201 million years ago to 66 million years ago. These bullet-shaped, squid-like animals lived close to shore in shallower waters. They often show up in fossils because—unlike their modern relatives—their bodies included a solid skeleton. Their internal shell was split into three pieces. The

A model of a belemnite.
JAMES COSGROVE

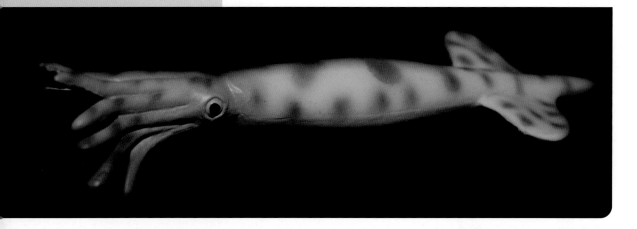

A collection of belemnite fossils.
PETER JOZEFEK/SHUTTERSTOCK.COM

solid tail section was known as the ***rostrum***. The largest known rostrum is about 18 inches (46 centimeters) long and was found in Indonesia. Their name, belemnite, comes from a Greek word meaning "dart," because that's what the rostrum looks like. The biggest belemnites were likely about 16 feet (5 meters) long. They had 10 tentacles with hooks made of chitin. They also had ink sacs—and some of these ancient ink sacs are still intact.

INK SPOTS.

WHAT'S IN A NAME?

What a culture calls an animal often gives us a sense of their relationship with that animal. The people who called octopuses devil fish clearly thought octopuses were scary. Author David Scheel looked at the names octopuses were given by Indigenous nations on the west coast of North America for his book *Many Things Under a Rock*—the title is a rough translation of the Eyak word for octopus and also conjures a wonderful image. The Eyak's traditional territory is located in what's now known as central Alaska. David noted that the words for octopus from the Łingít, Haida and Ts'msyen Peoples who live along the Northwest coast of North America are all variations of words for bait, because octopus makes excellent bait. The Swedish name for octopus translates as ink fish. The Danish name basically means "spurting ink." One of the older German words means "sea spider" and tends to be used for all cephalopods.

A common octopus hides behind a den of collected shells.
MADELEIN WOLFAARDT/SHUTTERSTOCK.COM

5
OCTOPUS GARDENS

For most mollusks, home is where the shell is. Since octopuses don't have shells, they find and make their own homes. Until recently it seemed likely the only octopus garden was in a Beatles' song. Then, in 2013, the first octopus nursery— with over 100 brooding octopus moms— was found off the coast of Costa Rica, just over 9,000 feet (2,800 meters) under the water. A second nursery was discovered nearby. A third nursery was discovered in Nuu-chah-nulth waters not far from Hesquiat Harbour off the coast of Vancouver Island. A fourth is located

"They are definitely our fellow earthlings and some of the oddest ones that we share the planet with."

—Danna Staaf, author

An octopus garden.
PHOTO COURTESY OF SCHMIDT OCEAN INSTITUTE

A common octopus is blending shape and color to match the white and black of the coral in front of their den.
MADELEIN WOLF/GETTY IMAGES

near Monterey, California. As humans keep exploring the seas with better diving equipment and higher-quality cameras, I'm sure that more octopus gardens will be discovered.

OCTOPOLIS AND OCTLANTIS

There are (at least) two sites off the coast of eastern Australia where the gloomy octopus—the name of this species was inspired by their large, sad-looking eyes—lives in the octopus equivalent of apartment complexes. These octopuses find their own holes to call home and pretty much mind their own business. Researchers have dubbed these communities Octopolis and Octlantis. Both areas have lots of places for an octopus to make a home and plenty of the animals who octopuses like to eat—including each other.

Octopuses generally live alone in almost any place they can squeeze into. Their homes are known as *dens*. Some octopuses move into discarded bottles. Bear homes are also known as dens, but there is no evidence of bears and octopuses ever becoming roommates. (I'd watch that cartoon, though.) One way to spot an octopus den is to look for piles of the empty shells of the animals they eat. These trash piles, known as *middens*, are often stacked outside their homes. Octopuses keep the inside of their den clean, but the outside looks like the undersea equivalent of a yard with an abandoned car or two on the lawn.

MATING DANCE

Octopuses don't do romance. Octopus arms have a lot of purposes, and the third right arm of a male octopus helps with reproduction, passing a package of sperm to the female but not creating it. So, like most aspects of octopus anatomy, it's complicated. The octopus creates the sperm inside his body. This special arm is known as the **hectocotylus** and is one way humans determine the sex of an octopus.

A female octopus can save the sperm of a male for months before laying her eggs and fertilizing them. Different types of octopuses have different approaches to finding mates. The female *Bolitaena pygmaea* develops a glowing yellowy ring around her mouth when she's ready to mate. These octopuses grow to about two inches (less than five centimeters), and their eyes are on stalks.

Most octopuses don't live long—one to two years is a common lifespan. Some types are only around for about six months. For octopuses mating is the beginning of the end. Male octopuses die soon after mating and female octopuses don't last long after giving birth.

A giant Pacific octopus egg hatches.
JAMES COSGROVE

These day octopuses are mating.
DIVEIVANOV/GETTY IMAGES

INK SPOTS.

OCTOPUS FRIENDS

Octopuses eat each other, so they are not social animals. At least, most of them aren't. One species, first recorded off the waters of Nicaragua in the late 1960s, behaves so differently that it's legendary. These octopuses don't just play well with others, they share dens. They even mate differently than other octopuses. They look at each other. Until 2015 many scientists thought they were a myth and were known as the nameless wonder. They now have a name: the larger Pacific striped octopus.

Giant Pacific octopus eggs.
JAMES COSGROVE

OCTOPUS EGGS

Octopuses lay a lot of eggs. Some species lay as many as 200,000. But generally only a couple of the eggs survive. The strings of eggs they carry and care for are known as **clutches**. The length of time it takes for eggs to hatch depends on the species, the depth of the water and the temperature. Some eggs hatch in just two months. Once they lay their eggs, the mothers care for them. Looking after their young is called **brooding**. Mothers blow water over their eggs so they get enough oxygen. This also keeps the strings of eggs separate so they can hatch. The longest known brooding period for an octopus is more than four years. Octopuses do not eat while brooding. One way to divide types of octopuses is by the size of their eggs. There are big-egg octopuses—who can be little as adults— and little-egg octopuses—who can be big as adults. The red octopus is about the size of an adult human's fist. A red octopus mom lays eggs the size of multivitamins, and when they hatch they stay on the bottom of the ocean. A giant Pacific octopus lays about 68,000 tiny eggs.

BABY OCTOPUSES

Baby octopuses are almost transparent when they're born. They already have a few chromatophores. When they hatch, they are about the size of a grain of rice and known as *paralarvae*. Paralarvae use their very short arms to swim toward the surface, then drift just below the water. They eat zooplankton until they're a bit bigger than a sunflower seed. Then they sink and start their lives as juvenile octopuses. Even paralarvae can use ink and have fully functional eyes, chromatophores, beaks and, of course, arms. Young octopuses grow up fast, doubling their weight almost every week. Octo moms don't survive long after their offspring are born. As their bodies decompose, they attract the attention of potential predators and keep them clear of their newborns.

INK SPOTS.

SENESCENCE

At the end of his life, a male octopus starts to eat less, lose coordination and wander—apparently aimlessly. This is known as *senescence*. Octopuses don't survive long once they reach senescence—both because of their lack of control and the fact that a disoriented octopus is easy to catch. Octopus mothers waste away from starvation as they wait for their eggs to hatch.

A common octopus underwater off the coast of Spain.
CAVAN IMAGES/GETTY IMAGES

6

OCTOPUS CELEBRITIES

Octopuses are famous for getting in and out of pretty much anything. The only part of their body that can't squeeze through the smallest of openings is their beak—and their beak is pretty small. If they need to escape a predator—or a tight spot—they can leave an arm behind. A healthy octopus will regrow that missing arm in two to four months. This is known as regeneration and is a superpower shared by Marvel heroes like Deadpool and Wolverine. That severed arm may not stop moving for a while. Some believe these detached

> "They are not some slimy, gross monster. They are super smart. They are superheroes with superpowers."
>
> —Sy Montgomery, author, on the *Skaana* podcast

octopus arms will search for food and try to share it with their missing mouth.

Octopuses can change colors and textures to blend into their environments. They can even crawl on land. Some can survive out of the water for up to 30 minutes if they want to. But why would they want to? The key to their wild escape skills is their ability to problem-solve. Octopuses plot escape routes like master criminals in action movies.

ON THE LOOSE

One of the earliest octopuses studied by scientists was in an aquarium in Brighton, England, in 1873. He was caught escaping from his tank and reaching into other tanks to snack on the other specimens. We'll call him "the marauding rascal" because his captors did. This is from a report published in 1875: "The marauding rascal had occasionally issued from the water in his tank, and clambered up the rocks, and over the wall into the next one; there he had helped himself to a young lump-fish, and, having devoured it, returned demurely to his own quarters by the same route, with well-fed stomach and contented mind." In the 1920s an aquarium in Naples, Italy, also reported incidents of roving octopuses leaving their tanks to visit and eat their neighbors.

In the 1980s rare fish kept disappearing from Boston's New England Aquarium. The mystery was solved when a researcher showed up early for work and discovered an octopus looming over a tank of rare fish. This octopus would sneak out of their

INK SPOTS.

OCTOPUS GODS

The Hawaiian god Kanaloa—god of the oceans and long-distance sea voyages—was known to take the form of an octopus. The Ainu of Japan also have an octopus god. This octopus began life as a giant spider who attacked a village. When the villagers prayed to be saved, the sea god turned the spider into a god of the bay.

tank, slide three feet (just under a meter) along the floor, scale the other tank to grab a snack and then return home. In 2011 a giant Pacific octopus at the Seattle Aquarium was caught on camera sneaking into the shark tank to snack on dogfish.

DOWN THE DRAIN

At New Zealand's Marine Studies Centre in Dunedin, a New Zealand octopus named Sid discovered how to open his tank's plastic doors. Caught when he was about nine months old, Sid had been in the aquarium for only a few months before he found his way to the drains that pumped seawater into the aquarium tanks. He made his way there several times and once spent five days in a drain. When Sid was returned to his tank—with increased precautions to prevent further escapes—he made his way out again. He also attempted multiple escapes while his tank was being cleaned. Sid was eventually returned to the ocean.

Inky, another New Zealand octopus, pulled off an even more impressive escape. Found in a crayfish pot by a fisherman, the small octopus looked rough when he arrived at the National Aquarium of New Zealand. One night in 2016, while his tank was being cleaned, Inky crossed the floor, slipped into a 6-inch-wide (15-centimeter) drainpipe and made his way home to the Pacific Ocean. The only

Inky the octopus.
NATIONAL AQUARIUM OF NEW ZEALAND

clue Inky left to where he'd gone was a slimy trail of water. The part of this story that boggles my mind: Did he know that the pipe he chose went directly back into the ocean? If so, how?

INK SPOTS.

RAMBO THE OCTOGRAPHER

In 2015 a female octopus named Rambo—after the mopey macho movie character played by Sylvester Stallone—learned how to use a waterproof camera. The octopus lived on display at SEA LIFE Kelly Tarlton's Aquarium in Auckland, New Zealand, and took photos of tourists. According to her trainer, it took Rambo just three tries to learn to take a photo when a visitor pressed the buzzer to request one. This octopus didn't become very famous, but I think she should have, since she may be the first and only octopus artist.

Rambo ready to take a photo.
COURTESY OF SEA LIFE KELLY TARLTON'S AQUARIUM

ESCAPE AT THE SALISH SEA CENTRE

The Salish Sea Centre had its own impressive escape artist in 2013. Its octopus-in-residence had just finished her six-month stint on display and was about to return home when her replacement arrived early. The new octopus was placed in a holding tank in the backstage area of the aquarium. The tank was covered with a heavy lid and dive weights to hold down each corner.

One morning a volunteer arrived to feed all the animals and noticed that the floor was wet. They assumed the water was from a diving suit because all the tanks looked perfectly normal. As the volunteer walked up a ramp into the public part of the center, an octopus arm poked up to greet them. After they got over the shock, they took the octopus and returned her to her tank. The lid and the weights were still in place. The new octopus had clearly pushed the lid open and slithered out, and the tank lid closed behind her. The aquarium decided that after pulling off the perfect magic act, the octopus needed a magical name. Hundreds of visitors decided to name her after the *Harry Potter* hero Hermione.

Paul the Octopus selects Spain.
ROLAND WEIHRAUCH/GETTY IMAGES

THE PSYCHIC SOCCER OCTOPUS

Until *My Octopus Teacher*, the most famous cephalopod celebrity was a common octopus (*Octopus vulgaris*) who seemed to know more about FIFA World Cup soccer than any human expert. Pulpo Paul lived in the aquarium at Sea Life Oberhausen, Germany, which was staffed by soccer-loving humans. In 2010 the two-year-old octopus was offered a choice between two transparent glass containers, one decorated with Germany's national flag, the other with the upcoming opponent's flag. Both containers contained a treat—a mussel. The first container Paul chose was considered his prediction of which team would win.

Paul made headlines—and ruled social media—around the world as he kept picking the winner in Germany's matches. As Paul became more famous, angry fans would threaten to kill him when he predicted their team was going to lose. Some fans in Berlin sang songs attacking Paul. Leaders of countries Paul picked as winners offered

The Tellaro octopus.

the octopus protection. There's a Chinese movie—a thriller—inspired by Paul's story.

"Paul amazed the world by correctly predicting the winners of all Germany's World Cup clashes, and then of the final," said aquarium manager Stefan Porwoll. A memorial statue of him holding a soccer ball was set up in the aquarium. He was cremated and his ashes were placed inside a soccer ball. A section of the museum features newspaper headlines, gifts he was sent and even an eight-armed soccer jersey.

ITALY'S OCTOPUS HERO

There are a lot of legends about octopuses as monsters, but the people in Tellaro—considered one of Italy's most beautiful small towns—celebrate an octopus hero. According to the legend of the "polpo campanaro" (the bell-ringer octopus), in 1660 a Saracen pirate was set to attack the town with his crew. In one version of the story, Tellaro

The town of Tellaro, Italy, where the legend of the "polpo campanaro" originated.

was fogged in, and the person on watch in the bell tower was asleep. In another, the people were celebrating and no one noticed pirates approaching. Both stories have the same happy ending. A giant octopus stretched an arm out of the bay—or left the bay to climb up the bell tower—to ring the bell of the Church of San Giorgio. The townsfolk spotted the pirates, saved their home and have honored octopuses ever since. There's a plaque on the church that shares this story. Awesome octopus art is everywhere in Tellaro—on and in buildings and homes. The octopus is officially celebrated the second Sunday of August with a feast where the main meal is octopus.

INK SPOTS.

DOCTOR OCTOPUS

The most famous fictional octopus fights Spider-Man. Doctor Octopus is one of Spidey's original enemies, and although the character's origin story changes over the years, Doc Ock is pretty much always a scientific genius with eight metallic arms that sometimes have minds of their own. And every version of Doctor Octopus shows just how dangerous and tricky an eight-armed opponent can be.

ACADEMY AWARD® NOMINEE
BEST DOCUMENTARY FEATURE

BAFTA WINNER DOCUMENTARY

PRODUCERS GUILD OF AMERICA AWARD WINNER OUTSTANDING PRODUCER OF DOCUMENTARY MOTION PICTURES

MY OCTOPUS TEACHER

"SHE MADE ME REALIZE JUST HOW PRECIOUS WILD PLACES ARE."

WINNER PARE LORENTZ AWARD IDA DOCUMENTARY AWARDS

WINNER BEST MUSIC SCORE KEVIN SMUTS IDA DOCUMENTARY AWARDS

WINNER BEST SCIENCE/NATURE DOCUMENTARY CRITICS' CHOICE DOCUMENTARY AWARDS

WINNER BEST CINEMATOGRAPHY ROGER HORROCKS CRITICS' CHOICE DOCUMENTARY AWARDS

WINNER GRAND TETON AWARD JACKSON WILD MEDIA AWARDS

"Absolutely unbelievable. **ONE OF THE BEST MOVIES EVER.**"
Jane Goodall, PhD, DBE, Founder
The Jane Goodall Institute
and U.N. Messenger of Peace

"The year's most unexpected tearjerker is **A HEART-EXPANDING ADVENTURE.**"
VANITY FAIR

The poster for
the documentary
My Octopus Teacher.
SEA CHANGE PROJECT

Illustration by Greg Ruth

7
OCTOPUS TEACHERS

Would you like to hang out with an octopus in their home? That's what filmmaker Craig Foster did. As he was dealing with challenges in his life, Craig met an octopus who reignited his passion and his imagination. He snorkeled, so he was never far below the water, and filmed the octopus in a South African kelp forest near his home. His movie won the Academy Award for best documentary in 2021 and introduced people to the idea that octopuses are individuals with personalities.

> "A lot of people say an octopus is like an alien. But the strange thing is, as you get closer to them, you realize that we're very similar in a lot of ways."
>
> —Craig Foster,
> *My Octopus Teacher*
> (a documentary released in 2020)

INK SPOTS.

PET OCTOPUS

Danna Staaf, author of several books on octopuses and squid, had a pet octopus when she was 10. She was in love with octopuses, and not only bought a huge home for her buddy—a 60-gallon (230-liter) tank—but also made a point of keeping her friend, Serendipity, well fed and entertained. Some people around the world keep octopuses as pets in tanks in their homes. Because octopuses aren't endangered, many places that sell sea animals as pets can or will sell octopuses.

Octopus experts worry that home aquarium owners might harm the populations of some of the cuter and more exotic species we don't know much about, like the dumbo octopus. They also worry about someone being hurt if they adopt a poisonous blue-ringed octopus. A pet octopus isn't very expensive, but it costs a lot to manage a tank that an octopus can't escape from or break. You can't just buy octopus chow at the mall. Octopuses like their food alive. Even healthy octopuses don't live long, and

when they reach senescence they die quickly. Danna says Serendipity and her second octopus each lived for less than a year, and that's one reason she decided not to get a third octopus.

Octopuses are used to having entire oceans to explore. An aquarium like the Salish Sea Centre has large tanks with interesting designs, and staff who do what they can to keep their octopus entertained. People who live with dogs know they have to walk them. An octopus needs a lot more care than a fish.

One of the best ways to meet animals is on-screen, and some movies change the way the world sees them. *My Octopus Teacher* is one of those movies. When I was hanging out at the Salish Sea Centre, almost all the volunteers told me that guests were constantly asking questions inspired by *My Octopus Teacher*. The movie didn't just change the way people see and treat octopuses—it meant that discoveries about octopuses became "news."

THE *OCTOPUS TEACHER* EFFECT

In 2013 the documentary *Blackfish* debuted and convinced people around the world that keeping orcas in captivity

A baby octopus hangs on to filmmaker Craig Foster's wristwatch.
SEA CHANGE PROJECT

This shot of an octopus just above the ocean floor is from *My Octopus Teacher*.

was wrong. The change in attitudes and the anti-captivity activism that followed became known as "the *Blackfish* effect." Other environmentally themed movies have changed the way people see the natural world. *Sharkwater* sparked worldwide protests against the practice of killing sharks for their fins.

I use the term "the *Octopus Teacher* effect" for the impact that movie had on the way people see cephalopods. When people think of octopuses now, they often view them through the lens of that documentary, in which the octopus was portrayed as clever and cuddly.

A 2023 survey showed that almost one in four Americans felt it was immoral to eat an octopus. Before *My Octopus Teacher* appeared on Netflix, it's possible that 25 percent of Americans might have found the idea of eating an octopus gross, but immoral? Jennifer Mather—who was the scientific consultant on the documentary—agrees it's likely

INK SPOTS.

ANTHROPODENIAL

By not naming the octopus star of his movie, Craig Foster tried to avoid doing something that a lot of scientists consider unscientific—anthropomorphizing. This is the term for suggesting an animal might have the same feelings or characteristics a human does. For many scientists, naming an animal is taboo—which seemed silly enough before we

animals, like dolphins, appear to have names for each other and that others, like bats, recognize each other's voices.

Some humans, especially human scientists, try not to admit that any other animal might be like us in any way. Claiming an animal might love or laugh or feel sad is known as anthropomorphizing. In 2001 Dutch scientist Frans de Waal came up with

feelings, emotions or intelligence: **anthropodenial**. The octopus in *My Octopus Teacher* made the same choice our friends do. She decided to spend her time with the human visitor with a camera and snorkel. She found him interesting enough to risk her safety by leaving her den and even attaching her body to his. Why? We don't know why our friends like us either.

that many of the people opposed to eating them only reached this conclusion after meeting the adorable little "teacher" on their screens.

OCTOPUS STUDIES

When I wrote about whales, there were dozens of other books for younger readers. There are hundreds of books about sharks. There are almost none about octopuses. That's changing fast. Since audiences visited that South African kelp forest in *My Octopus Teacher*, humans around the world haven't just become more interested in octopus but have also begun caring about how they're treated. If American laws shift to recognize octopuses as animals, not things, that would be the *Octopus Teacher* effect.

There are still not a lot of octopus movies. When I searched streaming sites, almost the only things that popped up after *My Octopus Teacher* were a few episodes of nature specials, the Korean drama series *Squid Game* and the cartoon *SpongeBob SquarePants*. There are also a few movies with evil octopuses who have the impressive ability to roar—something a real octopus can't do because they don't have voice boxes. I suspect we'll be seeing a lot more octopus movies soon—focusing on how amazing they are.

Craig Foster meets a curious octopus in a scene from *My Octopus Teacher*.

Dr. Sylvia Earle checks out an octopus on an underwater reef.

DANCING WITH OCTOPUSES

My Octopus Teacher showed the growth of the relationship between a human and an octopus, and there is plenty of proof that octopuses recognize individuals. In 1959 scientists shared the story of Charles, a common octopus who was not keen on being experimented on. Instead of pulling a lever that would deliver food and turn a light on, he decided to spray the researcher with water. Charles finally ended the experiment when he pulled the lever out of the wall. In 2002 an octopus at the Point Defiance Aquarium in

Tacoma, Washington, would look out at viewers and then head toward the person who did most of the feeding. In 2005 a scientist reported that an octopus had singled out one particular night guard as a target for soaking with spray.

For her 2015 book *The Soul of an Octopus*, Sy Montgomery spent three years getting to know four different octopuses who lived at the New England Aquarium in Boston—Athena, Octavia, Kali and Karma— and shared stories of her relationships with them.

Legendary ocean explorer Sylvia Earle was in a submarine about 1,500 feet (just over 450 meters) underwater when she spotted a female octopus holding her eggs. The explorer moved the submarine away from the octopus. The octopus moved with her. As the submarine changed directions, the octopus did too—as if they were playing. She described the experience—which lasted about an hour—as dancing with the octopus.

A diver meets an ornate octopus off the waters of Hawaii.
DR. DWAYNE MEADOWS/NOAA/CC BY 2.0

In 2018 scientists at Johns Hopkins University gave a pair of two-spot octopuses a drug commonly known as Ecstasy. The animals had pretty much the same reactions to it as humans do. The test confirmed a finding that the brain chemicals responsible for behavior are similar in humans and octopuses. Humans are known to become friendlier— and huggier—on Ecstasy, and the octopuses did too.

A giant Pacific octopus stretches out in the Sea of Japan.
ANDREY NEKRASOV/GETTY IMAGES

8
EIGHT AMAZING OCTOPUSES

Here are eight amazing octopuses. There are more than 300 octopus species in total, so you may have a different favorite.

THE GIANT PACIFIC OCTOPUS

There are a few reasons why this is the go-to aquarium octopus. Because of how often they're seen and how many eggs they lay, they are not believed to be endangered or even scarce. They are found throughout the Pacific Ocean. They can live in deep water—as deep

"We've got to lose this arrogance that just because we've got a brain that can design a rocket to go to Mars that doesn't mean that we have any more right to be on this planet than an octopus. We need to realize that we're part of this natural world and our lives depend on it."

—Jane Goodall, primatologist, environmental leader

as 4,900 feet (1,500 meters)—and near the shoreline in shallows like tide pools.

They are the largest octopus species, and when it comes to aquarium exhibits, bigger tends to be better. They become large quickly. They eat 20,000 calories a day and are one of the fastest-growing animals. They are generally colorful. Their default look is a light red. Their fave foods are shellfish like crabs and lobsters, but they're not fussy and have even been known to eat birds. A full-grown giant Pacific octopus may have more than 2,000 suckers. Just one of the suckers on a full-grown male can be around 3 inches (about 7.5 centimeters) in diameter and lift 30 pounds (just under 14 kilograms). Giant Pacific octopuses start out very tiny. They hatch from eggs the size of a drop of water.

THE NOT-SO-GIANT WOLFI OCTOPUS

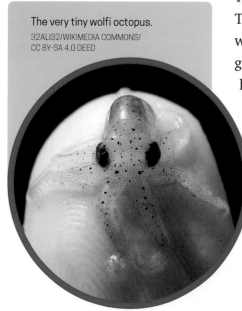

The very tiny wolfi octopus.
32ALI32/WIKIMEDIA COMMONS/
CC BY-SA 4.0 DEED

The smallest octopus in the world is believed to be the wolfi, or star sucker pygmy. They are about the size of one giant Pacific octopus sucker. A full-grown wolfi is less than half an inch (about a centimeter) long and weighs almost nothing. They live in the Indo-Pacific Ocean, where they float on the water and eat plankton for the first few months of their lives. Then they move underwater to the reef, where they eat tiny crustaceans. They don't live long—about six months—but unlike their larger relatives, who die shortly after giving birth, they are known to have as many as three clutches of eggs. Maybe there's a smaller species out there, but we haven't found it yet.

INK SPOTS.

THE BEAST

The largest confirmed giant Pacific octopus—the one in the *Guinness Book of World Records*—was caught near my home in Victoria, British Columbia, and displayed not far from where I live. Known as the Beast, he weighed 156 pounds (just over 70 kilograms) and measured more than 22 feet (7 meters) from arm tip to arm tip. James Cosgrove, who wrote the book *Super Suckers: The Giant Pacific Octopus and Other Cephalopods of the Pacific Coast*, spent time with the Beast. He warned me that while I may find stories of larger octopuses out there, none of them are confirmed to have been weighed or measured, and some were likely squid.

He also noted that these octopuses behave differently depending on which part of the Pacific they call home and what predators might be looking to eat them. Alaskan giant Pacific octopuses are more likely to hang out under rocks close to the surface because that's a good place to hide from sea otters. BC waters don't have many sea otters—though the climate crisis may change that.

THE KILLER OCTOPUS

The octopus who is deadliest to us is also one of the smaller members of the species—the blue-ringed octopus. They are covered with glowing bright-blue rings and take down their prey with one of the world's deadliest natural poisons, which is in their saliva. They eat crabs and shrimp—not us—but you don't want to get close enough to one to test their poison. These shy, nocturnal octopuses really aren't interested in attacking us. Bites are rare enough that there are only three confirmed human deaths caused by blue-rings. There are at least four different species of blue-ringed octopus, and scientists suspect there are more. The biggest of these is smaller than a grapefruit. Like many poisonous animals, this octopus is colorful and hangs out near Australia.

A deadly blue-ringed octopus hangs out off the waters of Indonesia.
HAL BERRAL/GETTY IMAGES

A mototi octopus carries a tiny crab on the seabed near Indonesia.

TOMMI KOKKOLA PHOTOGRAPHY/GETTY IMAGES

The only other octopus with poison this deadly is the mototi octopus—another tiny member of the family who is mostly found near French Polynesia. Also known as the poison ocellate octopus, they have also been found near Japan, Indonesia and, of course, Australia.

MASTER OF DISGUISE

Mimic octopuses don't just change their color and skin texture—they shift their arms and transform their bodies to look like other animals. The great undersea impersonators, mimic octopuses can disguise themselves as more than a dozen different species, including anemones, jellyfish, crabs, snakes, seahorses, stingrays and various types of fish. They even copy the way these species move. Found on the bottom of riverbeds off the waters of Indonesia, this awesome octopus was only discovered by scientists in 1998.

THE RULE BREAKER

The paper nautilus, or argonaut, is an octopus who seems to exist to break octopus rules. The paper nautilus also breaks nautilus rules—because, despite the name, they're not a nautilus. Most octopuses swim solo, but the paper

A mimic octopus in the waters off Indonesia.

BERNARD RADVANER/GETTY IMAGES

nautilus is known to travel in groups. Females sometimes join other females to float in octopus chains. They've also been known to catch rides on other sea animals—like jellyfish—and pieces of wood.

Most octopuses are big on hiding. The paper nautilus is pelagic and hangs out at the ocean surface. Most octopuses don't have shells. The paper nautilus does. Unlike other octopuses, who hide their eggs, female paper nautiluses create a thin shell to hold their eggs. A *lot* of eggs. Mom carries and guards about 170,000 eggs. While female octopuses are generally bigger than males, the female paper nautilus is about eight times bigger and weighs 600 times more than the male does. These octopus outliers live in tropical waters in the Pacific, Atlantic and Indian Oceans and eat plankton, mollusks and other small ocean animals. They are a favorite food of dolphins, tuna and other fish. They live for about a year.

A dumbo octopus in the Gulf of Mexico. Doesn't this look like an octopus plush toy?

EXPN2379/NOAA/CC BY-SA 2.0 DEED

A flapjack devilfish (how's that for a name?) floating in US waters.

NOAA/WIKIMEDIA COMMONS/ CC BY-SA 2.0 DEED

ADORABLE OCTOPUSES

The dumbo octopus is named after the Disney cartoon elephant with oversized ears. These octopuses don't have epic earlobes, but their earlike fins resemble them enough to have sparked the silly name. They use these fins to move through the water and have webbed arms that work a bit like sails for steering. They look more like plush toys than predators. They have been described as "adorable" and "the cutest octopuses in the world."

Dumbos live near the bottom of tropical to temperate seas. They can hang out at depths of 13,000 feet (4,000 meters) or perhaps even farther down—humans haven't spent much time checking out ocean floors. Looking for middens of discarded shells outside a den is usually a good way to find most octopus species, but this doesn't work with dumbos because they eat shells.

Dumbos don't have ink. The theory for why is that they never needed this protection because they don't

ANMUELLE/GETTY IMAGES

run into many predators living as deep in the ocean as they do. They eat snails, worms and other small animals who live on ocean floors. Like other deep-sea octopuses, their suckers have a bonus feature—hairlike "fingers" made of tissue, called *cirri*. These are likely used for sensing chemicals and other parts of their world.

The scientific name for their genus (kind) is *Grimpoteuthis*—which sounds like a fine name for a Disney villain. Most dumbos are around 8 to 12 inches (20 to 30 centimeters). Since their ocean-floor home makes it tough to find them, it's possible that jumbo dumbos are out there somewhere—possibly refusing to show themselves until someone gives them a more respectable name.

A drifting, or pelagic, octopus.
PHOTO COURTESY OF SCHMIDT OCEAN INSTITUTE

INK SPOTS.

OCTOPUS OF GLASS

The beautiful glass octopus is pretty much transparent in deep water and invisible to predators and prey.

A glass octopus floats in the black ocean.
PHOTO COURTESY OF SCHMIDT OCEAN INSTITUTE

PELAGIC OCTOPUSES

Most octopuses live near the bottom of the ocean, but pelagic octopuses hang out closer to the surface—which makes them popular seafood for other ocean animals. Pelagic octopuses include the football octopus (one of the only cephalopods with a swim bladder), telescope octopus (who are transparent and glow in the dark) and the common blanket octopus. Blankets are another species in which the females are much bigger than the males. A male blanket octopus is about the size of a chicken egg. The females can grow to about six feet (two meters) across and have webbing between their arms (which is why they're known as blankets). They are found in the Atlantic and Pacific Oceans and Indo-Pacific waters.

WALKING OCTOPUSES

Coconut octopuses earned their name because they create their own home by covering their bodies with seashells and coconut shells. Averaging 6 inches (15 centimeters) in length and weighing 10.5 ounces (300 grams), these octopuses live in the shallow, calm waters of the Indian and Pacific Oceans, preferring bays, lagoons and shores to open ocean. Perhaps because of their clever survival strategy, they live longer than most of their cousins. A coconut's lifespan is about two years. Once they've covered themselves, they will use a pair of arms to walk on the ocean floor as if they're walking on two legs. Yes, really. When they're not changing colors, coconuts are orange to dark brown, and their suckers are white—which can make it look like they glow. They eat crabs, clams and shrimp.

INK SPOTS.

THE OTHER GIANT OCTOPUS

In 2017 researchers in Alaska discovered a second type of giant Pacific octopus. They look like the ones humans know well but have a frill that travels along their body and two white spots on their head instead of one. These frilled octopuses also have "eyelashes" of raised skin.

A coconut octopus checks out the world beyond the shell.
SERGEUWPHOTO/SHUTTERSTOCK.COM

Beware the kraken! A drawing from the 1887 book *Monsters of the Sea, Legendary and Authentic.*

9

The Kraken, Devil Fish and Alien Octopus

"Here there be dragons" was the warning on some ancient maps to mark uncharted or dangerous territories. Some of those maps showed dragons. Some showed octopuses or squid. One of the most legendary sea monsters was the kraken.

SEA MONSTERS

Scandinavian stories from about a thousand years ago blame this giant squid for attacking ships and eating sailors. The kraken was the unstoppable monster in early Norse sagas.

"If you believe such things, there's a beast does the bidding of Davy Jones. A fearsome creature with giant tentacles that'll suction your face clean off, and drag an entire ship down to the crushing darkness. The Kraken..."

—Joshamee Gibbs, in *Pirates of the Caribbean* (written by Ted Elliott and Terry Rossio)

75e ANNIVERSAIRE DE LA MORT DE
JULES VERNE

Poste Aérienne

Vingt Mille Lieues
sous les Mers

200F
REPUBLIQUE TOGOLAISE

198

PICTURELAKE/GETTY IMAGES

They were the size of islands and held huge schools of fish on their back. The beast was said to attack ships with their long arms and, if that failed, circle ships to create a whirlpool that would suck the boats and their crews to the bottom of the ocean. Around 1180 the king of Norway claimed he saw a kraken and lived to tell the tale. The stories warned that the monster lived and hunted in the open waters off Scandinavia. Oh, and in many versions of the story, they had horns. Fossilized tree resin found on beaches in the North Sea were identified as—um—kraken droppings.

This fearsome beast is one of the world's best-known sea monsters. France's Jules Verne featured the kraken as a deadly nemesis for his heroes. The octopus or the squid was the model for the invading aliens in the classic science fiction story *The War of the Worlds* by H.G. Wells.

ALIEN OCTOPUSES

You may have heard that scientists found proof that octopuses are aliens. As awesome as that might be, it's not exactly true. In 2015 scientists from the United States and Japan ran a test to determine the genetic makeup, or genome sequence, of a California two-spot octopus. They discovered that this sequence is unique and doesn't match with that of any other animal. Media around the world declared that scientists had called octopuses aliens, which they sort of did. But they weren't suggesting that octopuses are from outer space.

Different studies have shown that although the most distant shared ancestors of octopuses and humans—a kind of worm—haven't been connected in about

500 million years, we still have a few neurotransmitters in common.

Even though octopuses aren't aliens, their intelligence is so different from ours that the people who are trying to contact aliens wanted to study their minds. Canadian octopus expert Jennifer Mather was invited to explain octopus thinking to the SETI (Search for Extraterrestrial Intelligence) Institute because their intelligence is, well, alien from the way we've traditionally believed intelligence works. Humans always believed that species evolved their ability to think and reason due to relationships, families and community. Most species we consider smart also have teachers. But octopuses are smart and solitary.

DEVIL FISH

The name devil fish was used for any sea animal with an appearance that scared early fishers, so it included octopuses, squid, gray whales and rays. They were considered ugly, evil and dangerous. Monsters. A possible reason octopuses received the devil name is because some of them have bumps that look like horns—a traditional devil image. Devil fish like the octopus may have been an inspiration for the Gorgon—a mythological Greek monster with poisonous snakes for hair. According to legend, if someone sees the Gorgon's face, they turn to stone. Many images of the Gorgon and of Medusa, the Roman version of the same monster, look like a woman who has an octopus with extra arms on her head.

INK SPOTS.

SEATTLE KRAKEN

While there have been no confirmed sightings of kraken in the waters near Seattle, they've been seen on ice since 2019. When Seattle landed an NHL team, 1,200 possible names were considered before fans voted for the Kraken. Another contender was Sockeyes—a fave local salmon. "I think this name embodies a connection with the sea and a curiosity of what lies beneath it," Seattle Kraken general manager Ron Francis said when the name was announced. "It reflects the power and aggression in the game of hockey." In 2023, in only its second year in the NHL, the Kraken proved fierce enough to make it to the Stanley Cup semifinals.

JENN G/WIKIMEDIA COMMONS/CC BY-SA 2.0 DEED

A Caribbean reef squid at a
reef in Roatan, Honduras.

10

SQUID SQUADS

Squid have 10 limbs—eight arms and two tentacles—so that's why these octopus relatives are the stars of chapter 10. It's important to mention squid to make it clear that while they are similar to octopuses, they're not the same animal. Let's start with how to tell the difference between an octopus and a squid—besides just counting the number of limbs.

"How do you get a squid to laugh?" "Ten tickles."

—Author unknown (but it's in lots of joke books)

SWIMMING WITH SQUID

Tentacles are longer than arms, and a squid can keep them hidden in their

Danna Staaf in her squid hat.
DANNA STAAF

body until they need them. The end of a tentacle has a diamond-shaped pad tipped with teeth or hooks. When the two tentacles shoot out, they can lock together to trap prey.

Unlike octopuses, squid evolved for speed. A Humboldt squid can move at 15 miles (24 kilometers) per hour. American author Danna Staaf, who has written books about octopuses and squid, calls them "underwater rockets." While octopuses tend to find homes, squid are explorers who don't settle in dens. They swim faster than octopuses and most don't spend as much time crawling. Octopuses have almost no trace left of the shells of their ancestors. Squid and cuttlefish both have internal shells.

Once you get past all the arms, octopuses and squid still look very different. Octopuses generally have bigger, rounder bodies. Squid are shaped more like harpoons—triangular—and have a pair of fins. Squid eyes have circular pupils. Octopuses have rectangular pupils. There are around 300 types of each species.

They do have many of the same characteristics—the beak, the radula and a lot of suckers. And both species change colors and produce ink. Squid are more social and hang out with other squid, so you may find a school of squid or a squid squad. They hang out with squid who are about the same size since, like octopuses, they are cannibals.

INK SPOTS.

TENTACLES

How many tentacles does an octopus have? None. The eight limbs of an octopus are, officially, arms. Squid and cuttlefish have eight arms and two tentacles. They use the tentacles like legs and arms to hold and catch things. Arms and tentacles are both made of muscles and nerves and are covered with suckers, but the suckers don't go all the way down the tentacles.

GIANT SQUID

While a giant octopus can get pretty big, a giant squid can hit sea-monster size. The largest recorded giant squid weighed about a ton and was about 42 feet (13 meters) long. Their only known predator—besides us—is the sperm whale. Giant squid have the biggest eyes in the animal kingdom—they can grow to just under 10 inches (25 centimeters) in diameter—pretty much the size of a basketball. Humans have no clue how many giant squid are alive, how many species there are or where exactly they live because they've almost never been seen. It's suspected that they hunt alone, but we don't really know. Although sperm whales eat them, squid don't always go down easy, and sperm whales are often seen with sucker-shaped scars on their bodies.

OCTOPUS SQUID

Some big deep-sea squid glow in the dark—when they want to. *Taningia danae*, also known as the Dana octopus squid, basically have headlights that shine a bluish green. They are known as octopus squid because they have eight arms, which have rows of hooks that can retract like cat claws or octopus beaks. But they don't have tentacles. Instead there is a huge *photophore* (a light-emitting organ) at the end of two of their shorter arms. These photophores even have "eyelids" that open and close to control the light.

The maroon-colored squid aren't giant, but they are very big. They can grow up to seven feet (just over two meters) long and weigh more than 130 pounds (59 kilograms). They live in every ocean—but aren't found often. At least, not by us. Scientists aren't sure whether the lights are for catching prey, blinding predators, communication, or any or all of the above and more.

The body of a giant squid found in Norway in 1954.
NTNU VITENSKAPSMUSEET/WIKIMEDIA COMMONS/CC BY-SA 2.0 DEED

A cuttlefish swims in the Sea of Japan.
PANWASIN GETTI/GETTY IMAGES

INK SPOTS

BOBTAIL SQUID

These tiny nocturnal squid are **bioluminescent**, which means they glow. Found in the tropical waters of the central Indo-Pacific, the males are just over an inch (about three centimeters) long, and females grow to just under two inches (about five centimeters). Because cephalopods are amazing, they can shift their colors so that their glowing light mimics moonlight. In 2023 scientists at the Marine Biological Laboratory in Massachusetts revealed that they'd bred albino bobtail squid, a transparent species that allows researchers to see the animals' entire nervous system.

CUTTLEFISH SCHOOL SCIENTISTS

While there are some very small octopuses and squid, the tiniest members of the cephalopod family tend to be cuttlefish. In 2021 researchers were shocked when cuttlefish passed an intelligence test designed for humans that has been tried on only a few animals.

The marshmallow test was created to test self-control. Four-year-old children are given the chance to eat a single marshmallow right away or wait about 15 minutes and get an extra one. Humans younger than four don't tend to wait for marshmallow number two. Most kids four and older do.

WILDESTANIMAL/GETTY IMAGES

It's a challenging test to do on most animals, and not just because not every species likes marshmallows—even if they're perfectly toasted. So with other species it's all about finding their version of a tasty treat. Researchers tried this test on cuttlefish, using grass shrimp as the prize. When the cuttlefish passed the test, the results were considered shocking because they suggested not only the willingness to wait but the ability to reason. Cuttlefish can also understand numbers to (at least) five. Many humans have trouble wrapping their heads around how smart apes, elephants and orcas are let alone learning that an animal as uncomplicated as a cuttlefish can think.

A pair of Caribbean reef squid in waters near the Netherlands.
J.T. LEWIS/SHUTTERSTOCK.COM

INK SPOTS.

SQUID SQUADS

Modern researchers like Danna Staaf are trying to get people to refer to groups of squid as squads instead of schools. Not only is it a more fun and squid-specific term, but squid don't hang out together or navigate the same way fish do. "They're similar to a school of fish, but different," she told me. Danna explains that squid squads might move together, with some going forward and others going backward, because of the way they use jet propulsion.

Octopus being dried to be
sold as food in Greece.
GATSI/GETTY IMAGES

11

PREDATORS AND PREY

It's an octopus-eat-octopus world. One place octopuses are always popular is on a menu. They are eaten by almost everyone and pretty much everywhere. When I told people I was writing a book about octopuses, several of them joked, "Is it going to include recipes?"

Humans catch octopuses on purpose and accidentally. Traditional fishing methods include fish traps and spearfishing. Commercial fishers tend to use nets to go after a particular species but often scoop up anything around them. The animals caught unintentionally

"Octopuses are cannibals. Which means if you crowd two animals, you may end up with one very well-fed one."

—Jennifer Mather, octopus expert

A freshly cooked baby octopus.
PAUL ASMAN AND JILL LENOBLE/WIKIMEDIA COMMONS/CC BY-SA 2.0 DEED

Octopus-flavored potato chips for sale at a store in Canada.
MARK LEIREN-YOUNG

are known as *bycatch*—a harmless-sounding word for a very harmful and common practice. The fishers are accidentally (and sometimes not so accidentally) catching and killing endangered species and massive amounts of marine life they can't sell, and the dead animals are tossed back into the ocean.

EATING OCTOPUS

Just after one of my visits with Storm, I stopped in at Whole Foods and saw octopus arms on sale. Not only are all parts of an octopus edible, but some people eat them while the animal is still alive. Most people avoid eating the beak, ink sac and some internal organs, but that'd be tough to do if you were swallowing a small one while it's still squirming. Some people are big fans of eating the eyes. Many cultures consider the ink a delicacy.

I've never eaten octopus, but I gather one reason it's a popular food is that it absorbs the flavor of whatever it's cooked in—the way tofu and mushrooms do. Octopus is a healthy meal—rich in protein, vitamin B12, selenium and zinc. In most cultures people eat the suckers and the arms. In Japan diced octopus cooked in balls is a popular street food. They are also served as pancakes or flattened in a hot press and served as crackers. Octopus is a staple of sushi. In one South Korean dish, longarm octopus arms are still moving when they are served, even after being chopped up and sautéed in sesame oil. A popular street food is octopus cooked on sticks— Korean kebabs. Squid is also on a lot of menus and popular in fish-and-chip shops around the world.

OCTOPUS PREDATORS

Humans aren't the only animals who find octopus tasty. One reason octopuses need to be clever is that any animal who *can* eat an octopus will—and almost any animal can. Because of their lack of bones, octopuses are easy for other marine life to eat and digest. Squids are the same. "Squid are like the protein bars of the ocean," author Danna Staaf told me. "They have no hard parts. They have no bones, and they have no shell."

Among the animals who eat octopuses (besides us) are fish, seals, sea lions, otters, most toothed whales (like sperm and beaked whales), dolphins (who are also part of the whale family), eels and other octopuses—not just other species of octopus but other members of the same species, including family members. Birds, including gulls and albatrosses, also eat octopus. Octopuses may be able to hide, but they're not great at running away. When being chased, it doesn't take long before they get too tired to escape their predators.

INK SPOTS.

DO OCTOPUSES EAT HUMANS?

Octopuses can certainly become big and strong enough to attack and kill a human. But octopuses generally avoid us in the wild. The biggest danger when you're diving near an octopus is that they've been known to peel off dive masks, and octopuses can stay underwater a lot longer than we can. There's no evidence of any big octopus ever eating a human—so much for their reputation as sea monsters. Of course, they are brilliant, so maybe when they take out a human, they find a way to make it look like a shark did it.

Dolphins bite off their heads and toss their bodies into the air over and over to tenderize them. Hammerhead sharks use their fancy heads to hold octopus down before pulling them apart. Seals slap octopuses around on the surface of the water to kill them. Eels hide in reefs to attack and then wrap around them—like an octopus might wrap an arm around their prey. Sperm whales swallow them whole. Sometimes their predators just eat an arm or three. Humans often use octopus as bait because the muscle is tough and they are considered tasty by other undersea animals.

OCTOPUS FARMS

Is farming octopuses a way to save them or a cruel and unusual punishment for intelligent animals? Both? Or neither? Farming ocean animals—known as *aquaculture*—isn't new. Coastal communities in North America and Australia ran sustainable oyster fisheries for over 5,000 years. But the idea of commercial aquaculture—farming enough animals to sell not just to a single community but to other communities—is relatively new. And the idea of farming octopuses commercially is new and controversial.

When a Spanish company applied for a permit to farm 3,000 tons (2,720 metric tons) of octopus annually in 2023, people around the world protested. That amount is only a fraction of the amount of octopus people eat each year—which is estimated at roughly 400,000 tons (363,000 metric tons). "It's not just that it's a lousy thing to do to octopuses," Jennifer Mather told me. "It's also not going to work."

Boiled octopus on sale at a market in South Korea.

JUNHO JUNG/WIKIMEDIA COMMONS/ CC BY-SA 3.0 DEED

OCTOPUS RIGHTS

In recent years scientists have shown that animals, insects and even plants are smarter than most of us ever imagined. But what scientists have discovered about octopus intelligence has been so surprising that even people who aren't opposed to eating animals are opposed to farming them as food. In the United States and Canada, politicians are demanding that octopus farming be illegal. This isn't just because octopuses are smart—after all, pigs are very clever before they become bacon—but because they, unlike most animals, live solitary lives in open oceans. The reason aquariums have just one octopus in a tank at a time is that if you put a second octopus in the same space, they will fight to the death for the territory.

Many people working to free marine mammals like orcas and dolphins from captivity stress that these are social animals and keeping them in isolation and away from other orcas or dolphins is cruel. Forcing hundreds or thousands of solitary octopuses—or even two—into a confined space may be just as cruel.

Protesting a proposed octopus farm.
SOPA IMAGES LIMITED/ALAMY STOCK PHOTO

Divers and a giant Pacific octopus in the Sea of Japan.

OCTOPUS LAW

Researchers in favor of octopus farms claim they've created conditions in which octopuses can live together and thrive without attacking each other. They say they've even found ways to keep female octopuses alive after they've delivered one set of eggs, so they can reproduce as many as three times. They also claim to have found a more humane way to kill octopuses—by dropping the water temperature until they freeze to death. At sea, octopuses caught by fishers are generally clubbed, suffocated or stabbed. Right now there are almost no rules anywhere for how an octopus at a farm—or anywhere else—can or should be treated. No species of octopus is considered endangered, so none of them are protected by national or international laws designed to help endangered species.

OCTOPUS EXPERIMENTS

Scientific experimentation is one area in which octopuses and other cephalopods are protected—at least in some parts of the world. In 1991 the Canadian Council on Animal Care declared that they deserve the same respect as other animals. This means research needs to be approved, and if cephalopods are experimented on, scientists need to try to make it as painless as possible. In 2010 the European Union agreed that cephalopods should have the same protections as other animals. And in 2021 the United Kingdom declared that lobsters, crabs and octopuses are legally sentient—or thinking—beings who feel pain. This makes it easier to create laws to improve the way they're treated. An American study the same year confirmed that octopuses do feel pain. I'm sure scientists could have figured this out years earlier—if it was something people really wanted to know.

Scientists have experimented with anesthetics—medications that lessen pain—for octopuses and other cephalopods. This is a major challenge for an animal with so many nerve receptors. Canada, the United Kingdom, the European Union, New Zealand and some states in Australia have regulations to make sure cephalopods are treated with some care. The United States does not. While most researchers treat octopuses like they do other animals, the Federation of American Societies for Experimental Biology has fought regulations that would restrict the way they experiment on cephalopods. This likely has at least something to do with laws that allow scientists to cut off the animals' limbs to study regeneration. These laws are currently being revisited. The *Octopus Teacher* effect?

A small octopus checks out a diver.
DREWSULOCKCREATIONS/GETTY IMAGES

INK SPOTS.

WORLD OCTOPUS DAY

October 8 is the perfect day to celebrate octopuses. Think about it. The idea was first proposed in 2007 by the people who run the website TONMO.com—a forum for octopus fans. Some sites suggest celebrating by eating octopus—which seems a bit like declaring American Thanksgiving World Turkey Day.

An ornate octopus in
Hawaiian waters.
DR. DWAYNE MEADOWS/NOAA/CC BY 2.0

12
OCTOPUSES AND US

Storm was set to be released a few days after she shook my hand, but her return to the wild was delayed because the wild was on fire. The highway to her home off northern Vancouver Island was closed because of forest fires. The fires in western Canada were poisoning the air as far away as New York, on the other side of the continent. There have always been forest fires, but a predictable "fire season" is a new and terrifying phenomenon that we're seeing because of how humans have mismanaged the forests and the planet. Storm finally returned home

"Who would know more about the infinite, eternal ocean than an octopus?"

—Sy Montgomery
in her book *The Soul of an Octopus*

An octopus hangs off the arm of a diver.

about a month after her scheduled release, and she found herself facing many of the same challenges humans do—an ocean that's full of plastics and poisons.

COUNTING CEPHALOPODS

How many octopuses are there? We don't know. Right now it's pretty much impossible to accurately count them or even make a truly educated guess. So we don't know which octopus species might be endangered. Since they're stuck on the same planet as us—unless they really *are* aliens waiting to hitch a ride home—octopuses are facing the same threats we are.

The climate crisis and polluted oceans are destroying their habitat, which is also our habitat. There is so much plastic in the oceans that all of us are eating it.

Microplastics have been found inside pretty much every kind of animal on earth.

Octopuses can't fight the climate crisis or clean up the oceans by throwing shells. They can't stop pollution by changing color. That's up to us. Overfishing is happening pretty much everywhere—and the scary statistics that show this are based on legal fisheries. A lot of fishing happens illegally, which means the number of fish killed each year is severely underestimated. And the toxic chemicals we flush down toilets or toss out in other ways ultimately find their way into the water.

Yes, everyone can help save the ocean.

8 WAYS YOU CAN HELP SAVE OCTOPUSES, OCEANS AND US

SOLSTOCK/GETTY IMAGES

1 THINK ABOUT WHAT YOU BUY AND EAT

Eating in an environmentally friendly way is complicated. If you do eat octopus—or fish—try to find out whatever you can about what you're eating, like where and how the animal was caught. Today most of the bigger fish that people enjoy eating come with a side of mercury and a pinch of microplastics. Many sunscreens poison coral reefs. Choose sunscreens that don't kill coral. When you buy pretty much anything, think about packaging and potential waste.

2 CONSIDER WHAT YOU'RE THROWING "AWAY"

There is no "away." When we throw anything "away," it eventually ends up in the oceans. Humans make a big mess. North Americans are traditionally the world's winners when it comes to creating garbage. The less trash we each create, the better we're making the world for octopuses and us. So please try to limit what you throw out. One of the major sources of ocean plastic is "ghost gear"—fishing nets, longlines and other equipment that was cut loose or abandoned. Companies also dump poison into the water. Chemicals we stopped using decades ago are still poisoning the ocean. Octopuses and all marine life eat or absorb our medicines, pesticides, poisons and plastics. Medicines need to be properly disposed of. So do paints. So do all chemicals. Reduce. Reuse. Recycle. Repeat. Put the heat on corporations and politicians—which is where it belongs. The biggest polluters are big companies.

3 CONSIDER THE CLIMATE CRISIS

Climate change is making the earth a scarier place. One of the big dangers for marine life like octopuses is ocean acidification. Excess carbon dioxide makes water more acidic, which is killing sea life including coral and zooplankton—which is bad news for all the other animals in the water and on Earth. Climate change is increasing the range of some octopus species—but when animals shift habitats, their new homes tend to run out of either predators or prey and throw the ecosystem out of balance. Learn what you can do in your community to combat the climate crisis.

4 SHARE

Humans like to claim we're the only beings on the planet who are altruistic and can put the needs of others ahead of our own, but when we look at what we want to eat, we rarely worry about what other animals need to eat. Most human cultures tend to treat all other life on the planet as our food, our resources. Octopuses need to eat too. Imagine if we shared the world. Imagine how much more amazing the world would be.

5 END ANTHROPODENIAL

Animals aren't things. Octopuses may not be human, but don't pretend they're aliens. If an animal seems to be laughing, loving or in pain, assume they're laughing, loving or in pain. The idea that octopuses are "things" in the United States and have no protection in labs or lunches is horrifying. I'll share links to any campaigns to fight this on my website—www.leiren-young.com.

6 GET POLITICAL

Every community has environmental groups dealing with issues that affect the oceans. Find the issue that speaks to you and get involved. It doesn't matter how old you are—if you speak up, you can make a difference. Write letters, make calls, volunteer for causes that matter to you. Start your own movement. There are young eco-heroes around the world. Join them.

7 KEEP LEARNING ABOUT OCTOPUSES

One of my favorite internet tricks is setting news alerts so I get all the latest stories about animals who interest me. Set a news alert to get updates about your favorite octopus.

8 SHARE WHAT YOU LEARN

Don't be shy. People protect what they love. Share your favorite octopus facts. Tell your family. Tell your friends. Tell strangers. Create your own stories and books and movies and social media posts about octopuses. If you'd like to quote anything from this book on your favorite social media platform—or anywhere else—please do (though mentioning or linking to the book would make both my publisher and me happy). Passion makes a difference. Passion inspires people. You can inspire people.

GLOSSARY

anthropodenial—the belief that animals don't have feelings or emotions

aquaculture—the farming of ocean animals

bioluminescent—emitting light

brooding—protecting eggs until they hatch

bycatch—the fish or other sea life fishers accidentally or "accidentally on purpose" catch that they weren't fishing for

cephalopods—ocean-dwelling mollusks with strong, flexible arms and/or tentacles, including octopuses, squid and cuttlefish

chitin—the hard organic material that forms the shells of bugs and crabs and the beak of octopuses

chromatophores—tiny color-shifting organs in the skin of an octopus

chemotactic—a behavior in which an organism tastes food by touching it

cirri—slender projections made of tissue in the suckers of some deep-sea octopuses, there because…well, no one knows why yet

clutches—collections of eggs

dens—octopus homes

hectocotylus—the third right arm of a male cephalopod that assists in reproduction

invertebrates—spineless animals—almost every animal on earth

mantle—the body of an octopus, which almost everyone thinks is the head

melanins—pigments that create color in skin

middens—stacks of discarded shells in front of octopus dens

mollusks—invertebrates who live in the oceans. Cephalopods are all mollusks. There are freshwater mollusks too, but none of them are cephalopods.

nautilus—an ancient cephalopod with many slender tentacles and an external coiled shell similar to a snail's

octopi—not a real word, although most people think it's the plural of *octopus*; the plural is actually *octopuses*

papillae—the texture-shifting muscles of an octopus

paralarvae—newborn octopuses

pelagic—related to the open seas

photophore—a light-emitting organ

pseudomorph—an ink "bomb" that looks enough like a squid to fake out potential predators

radula—a sharp and versatile tongue

rostrum—the solid tail section of some undersea animals

senescence—the final phase of life of male octopuses, in which they become disoriented and start to die

siphon—the organ an octopus uses to shoot out water for propulsion and to flush out waste from the butt

statocysts—two small chambers found near the brain that help the octopus balance. They contain hairs that register vibrations, like human ears.

vampyropods—an ancient ancestor of octopuses and squid

PRINT

Montgomery, Sy. *The Octopus Scientists*. Clarion Books, 2015.

Montgomery, Sy. *Secrets of the Octopus*. Penguin Random House, 2024.

Staaf, Danna. *The Lady and the Octopus: How Jeanne Villepreux-Power Invented Aquariums and Revolutionized Marine Biology*. Carolrhoda Books, 2022.

ONLINE

American Oceans: americanoceans.org

Animal Fact Guide: animalfactguide.com/animal-facts/common-octopus

Britannica Kids: kids.britannica.com/kids/article/octopus/353559

Danna Staaf: dannastaaf.com

Kiddle: kids.kiddle.co/Octopus

LiveScience: livescience.com

Monterey Bay Aquarium: montereybayaquarium.org

National Geographic: nationalgeographic.org

National Geographic Kids: natgeokids.com/uk/discover/animals/sea-life/octopus-facts

Natural History Museum: nhm.ac.uk

National Wildlife Federation: nwf.org

Nature Conservancy Canada: natureconservancy.ca

Ocean Conservancy: oceanconservancy.org

OctoNation: octonation.com

Science Kids: sciencekids.co.nz/sciencefacts/animals/octopus.html

Schmidt Ocean Institute: schmidtocean.org

Sea History for Kids: seahistory.org/kids

Smithsonian Magazine: smithsonianmag.com

TONMO: The Octopus News Magazine Online: https://tonmo.com

DOCUMENTARIES

Ehrlich, Pippa, and James Reed, dirs. *My Octopus Teacher*. 2020; South Africa, Off The Fence and The Sea Change Project.

Geiger, Adam, dir. *Secrets of the Octopus*. 2024; United States, SeaLight Pictures.

PODCASTS

Skaana: skaana.org

ACKNOWLEDGMENTS

First off, I have to thank Storm. While I wish I'd met her more often—and that she'd found me and her surroundings more interesting—watching her and watching people watch her helped shape this book. I hope she had some grand adventures when she returned home to the ocean.

Thanks to Kit Thornton for introducing me to Storm and answering my questions. And thanks to the team at the Shaw Centre for the Salish Sea in Sidney, BC, for letting me meet their octopuses over the last few years.

Just before I started writing this book, I visited the 2022/2023 Divisions 11 and 14 classes taught by Morgan Holmes and Siri Hastings at Central Middle School in Victoria to ask the students what they knew about octopuses and what they wanted to know. Their questions helped inspire the stories I've included here.

Octopus experts Jennifer Mather and James Cosgrove generously talked me through all things cephalopod, then kindly agreed to read what I'd written to share their thoughts, comments and corrections. Danna Staaf, Warren Carlyle and Sy Montgomery made time to share their knowledge with me during (and after) lengthy interviews for the book, which were featured on the *Skaana* podcast.

Special thanks to the University of Victoria and especially one of my UVic students, Courtney Bill. I was lucky enough to receive funding for a student researcher for this book, courtesy of the VKURA Fellowship, and even luckier to connect with Courtney.

Courtney dove into the world of octopuses with me, and her research, discoveries and questions were invaluable. She not only helped track and confirm a lot of the information here, but also went on a fabulous fishing expedition to find many of the images featured in these pages. Courtney, Mika Ogilvie, Joan Watterson and Darron Leiren-Young were all kind enough to read early drafts and suggest corrections, fixes and improvements. I'm sure all errors are mine—except for errors in photo captions, which, I'm convinced, are caused by mischievous gremlins who attack books after they've gone to print.

Thanks to Bug Lewis for producing the *Skaana* podcast, which gave me the opportunity to speak with so many amazing people and share their stories with you here.

I will be forever grateful to Orca Book Publishers' Andrew Wooldridge and Ruth Linka for inviting me to keep swimming in the Orca pool and allowing me to dive into the world of these amazing animals. Thanks to editor Kirstie Hudson and editorial assistant Georgia Bradburne for all their advice and editing and designer Troy Cunningham for sharing the octopus and their environments on these pages. And thanks to everyone at Orca for all the stories they share with the world.

Above all, this book would not exist without the always awesome Rayne Benu—creator and executive producer of the *Skaana* podcast. Also my wife. As I was finishing my books on sharks for Orca, I wasn't sure which world to explore next. "Octopuses," she said. "You have to write about octopuses. They're amazing." She was right. As always.

And thank you for reading this. If you liked it, I hope you'll let other people know about this book and about these amazing (but not alien) animals.

EXPERT REVIEWS FOR
OCTOPUS OCEAN

"In the past, octopuses were thought to be horrible animals that were dangerous to anyone on or in the ocean; they were called 'devil fish.' Now we know that octopuses are incredible creatures. They are intelligent, problem-solving animals that often have very short lives. This book will introduce you to these fantastic animals and will leave you amazed at how they fill their place in nature."

—Jim Cosgrove, marine biologist and octopus researcher

"Mark Leiren-Young's *Octopus Ocean* gives young readers a wonderful sense of many aspects of the world of octopuses in a very clear, concise and interesting way. It makes the reader think, and it educates without preaching. This book is a door to the magnificent world of the octopus—a door that, if opened and explored, will bring much joy and connection."

—Craig Foster, producer of *My Octopus Teacher*, co-founder of the Sea Change Project

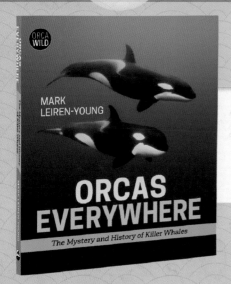

AGES 9-12

"The reader will certainly learn much about these fascinating, intelligent, and beautiful creatures, and hopefully will understand why they need to be protected."

—*School Library Connection*

"Dramatic photos, real-life stories, surprising facts, and ideas of how to help save sharks keep kids engaged...a fascinating introduction to an awe-inspiring animal that should be revered not feared."

—*Hakai Magazine*

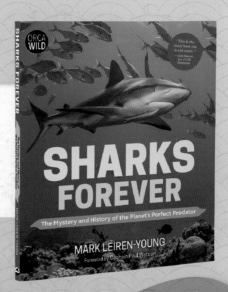

AGES 0-2

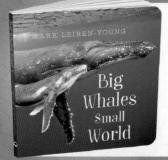

"Dynamic, real-life images of whales in their natural environment will mesmerize the youngest of readers, and the rhyming text is sure to capture their attention when read aloud."

—*CM: Canadian Review of Materials*

"So compelling that even non-shark lovers will find themselves gazing at the well-composed and vivid photos. This will be a book that will be requested often!"

—*School Library Journal*

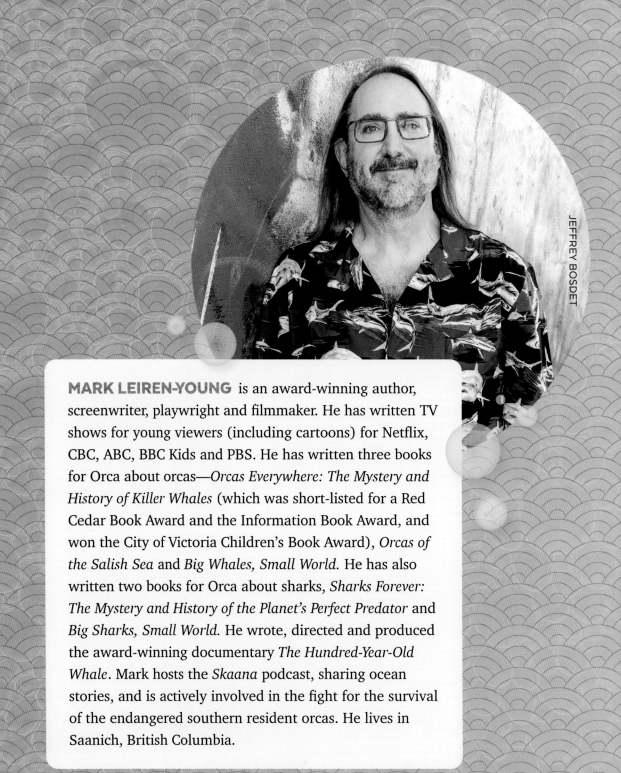

MARK LEIREN-YOUNG is an award-winning author, screenwriter, playwright and filmmaker. He has written TV shows for young viewers (including cartoons) for Netflix, CBC, ABC, BBC Kids and PBS. He has written three books for Orca about orcas—*Orcas Everywhere: The Mystery and History of Killer Whales* (which was short-listed for a Red Cedar Book Award and the Information Book Award, and won the City of Victoria Children's Book Award), *Orcas of the Salish Sea* and *Big Whales, Small World*. He has also written two books for Orca about sharks, *Sharks Forever: The Mystery and History of the Planet's Perfect Predator* and *Big Sharks, Small World*. He wrote, directed and produced the award-winning documentary *The Hundred-Year-Old Whale*. Mark hosts the *Skaana* podcast, sharing ocean stories, and is actively involved in the fight for the survival of the endangered southern resident orcas. He lives in Saanich, British Columbia.